D0866887

MODERN AMERICAN WIT & WISDOM

✳✳✳
✳✳✳

A Collection

MODERN AMERICAN WIT & WISDOM

***
***

A Collection

Compiled By

Anne Russell Wigton

STANYAN BOOKS

RANDOM HOUSE

A Stanyan book
Published by Stanyan Books,
8721 Sunset Blvd., Suite C
Los Angeles, California 90069,
and by Random House, Inc.
201 E. 50th Street,
New York, N.Y. 10022

Designed by Hy Fujita

Printed in U.S.A.

For Jay Allen

MODERN AMERICAN WIT & WISDOM

★★★
★★★

A Collection

One small step for man,
one giant step for mankind.

— Neil Armstrong

***
***

I cannot believe that God plays dice
with the Cosmos.

— Albert Einstein

Let the meek inherit the earth —
they have it coming to them.

— James Thurber

It is never too late to give up your prejudices.

— Henry David Thoreau

Publishing a column of verse is like
dropping a rose petal down the Grand Canyon
and waiting for the echo.

— *Don Marquis*

***
***

There is more pleasure in loving than
in being loved.

— *Thomas Fuller*

***
***

There are plenty of good five-cent cigars
in the country. The trouble is, they
cost a quarter.

— *Will Rogers*

***
***

It is a magnificent pedagogical challenge
to think about how you train people in 1970
for effective functioning in 1985, when no one
has the foggiest notion of what the world is
going to be like then.

— *Michael I. Sovern*

The best way to convince a fool that he
is wrong is to let him have his own way.

— *Josh Billings*

Life is a banquet and most poor sons of bitches
are starving to death.

— *Patrick Dennis*

✳✳✳
✳✳✳

After a quarter century of publication
I have learned never to discuss my work with a
fellow author. It excites them too much.

— *Gore Vidal*

New York has more hermits than will be
found in all the forests, mountains and
deserts of the United States.

          — *Simeon Strunsky*

Suburbia is where the builder bulldozes
down the trees, then names the streets
after them.

          — *Bill Vaughan*

And this is good old Boston,
  The home of the bean and the cod,
Where the Lowells talk to the Cabots,
  And the Cabots talk only to God.

          — *John Collins Bossidy*

If men knew how women pass the time
when they are alone, they'd never marry.

— *O. Henry*

***
***

It's not the kids, it's the parents.
The women of this country haven't risen up.
Dammit.

— *Adela Rogers St. Johns*

***
***

Woman would be more charming if one
could fall into her arms without falling
into her hands.

— *Ambrose Bierce*

***
***

A woman will buy anything she thinks a
store is losing money on.

— *Kin Hubbard*

The men with the muck-rake are often
indispensable to the well-being of society;
but only if they know when to stop
raking the muck.

> — *Theodore Roosevelt*

I consider anti-Semitism in America
as a possible criminal movement,
and every anti-Semite as a possible traitor
to America.

> — *Wendell L. Wilkie*

The church always arrives on the scene
a little breathless and a little late.

— *Bernard J. F. Lonergan, Jesuit*

*** ***

I don't believe in God because I don't believe
in Mother Goose.

— *Clarence Darrow*

*** ***

As a career, the business of an orthodox
preacher is about as successful as that
of a celluloid dog chasing an asbestos cat
through hell.

— *Elbert Hubbard*

*** ***

I must get out of these wet clothes
and into a dry martini.

> — *Alexander Woollcott*

Our whole civilization is based on a
hypothetical future and the idiocy of
fortune tellers.

> — *Stephen Vizinczey*

Trouble is a sieve through which we
sift our acquaintances. Those too
big to pass through are our friends.

> — *Arlene Francis*

Life is just one damned thing after another.

— *Frank Ward O'Malley*

It is not true that life is one damn thing after another; it's one damn thing over and over.

— *Edna St. Vincent Millay*

Only in America can you buy a lifetime supply of aspirin for one dollar, and use it up in two weeks.

— *John Barrymore*

I never knew a girl who was ruined by a book.

— *James J. Walker*

***

Adultery is democracy applied to love.

— *H. L. Mencken*

***

The ability to make love frivolously is
the chief characteristic which distinguishes
human beings from the beasts.

— *Heywood Broun*

***

O to be seventy again!

— *Oliver Wendell Holmes, Jr.*

***

Men who flatter women do not know them;
men who abuse them know still less.

— Mme. de Salm

*** ***
*** ***

Some of these people setting out to
clean up the world ought to start off
by taking a bath.

— Will Durant

*** ***
*** ***

To make money, buy some good stock,
hold it until it goes up and then sell it.
If it doesn't go up, don't buy it.

— *Will Rogers*

***
***

People who have never made or saved
a dollar are always letting me know
how to spend a million.

— *Henry Ford*

***
***

The two most beautiful words in the
English language are "check enclosed."

— *Dorothy Parker*

***
***

The only true gift is a portion of yourself.

— *Ralph Waldo Emerson*

***
***

Remember that bank I used to cry all the
way to? I bought it.

— *Liberace*

***
***

I will make a bargain with the Republicans;
if they will stop telling lies about the
Democrats, we will stop telling the truth
about them.

— *Adlai Stevenson*

***
***

Practical politics consists of ignoring the facts.

— *Henry Adams*

***
***

The Republicans have their split right
after election, and Democrats have theirs
just before an election.

— *Will Rogers*

***
***

I have never looked upon public office
as a form of social security.

> — *Sen. Edmund Muskie*

I not only use all the brains I have,
but all I can borrow.

> — *Woodrow Wilson*

You only live once, and if you play it right,
once is all you need.

— *Joe E. Lewis*

The game of golf consists of a lot of
walking, broken up by disappointment and
bad arithmetic.

— *Earl Wilson*

***
***

My father never raised a hand to any one
of his children, except in self defense.

— *Fred Allen*

***
***

I never make a move without first
ignoring my press agent.

— *Groucho Marx*

***
***

I am the oldest living man — especially
at seven in the morning.

— *Robert Benchley*

We usually meet all our relatives only at
funerals, where someone always observes,
"Too bad we can't get together more often."

— *Sam Levenson*

I want to be the white man's brother,
but not his brother-in-law.

— *Martin Luther King*

***
***

The American people never carry an
umbrella. They prefer to walk in the sunshine.

— *Alfred E. Smith*

***
***

The pious ones of Plymouth, reaching
the Rock, first fell upon their knees,
and then upon the aborigines.

— *William Evarts*

***
***

The best remedy for a cold is to go to bed with a good book, or a friend who's read one.

— *Rod McKuen*

***
***

There is nothing so stupid as an educated man, if you get him off the thing he was educated in.

— *Will Rogers*

***
***

Writing good editorials is chiefly telling people what they think, not what you think.

— *Arthur Brisbane*

***
***

Strip away the phony tinsel of Hollywood
and you find the real tinsel underneath.

— *Oscar Levant*

***
***

There are two things that will be believed
of any man . . . and one of them is that he
has taken to drink.

— *Booth Tarkington*

***
***

I don't regret anything I've ever done,
so long as I enjoyed doing it at the time.

— *Katherine Hepburn*

***
***

(On being interrupted by a train whistle
during an outdoor concert)
My gawd! Poifect pitch!

— Barbra Streisand

***

In Hollywood, a starlet is the name for
any woman under thirty who is not
actively employed in a brothel.

— Ben Hecht

***

I am not a little girl from a little town
making good in a big town. I am a big girl
from a big town making good in a little town.

— Mae West

***

There is this to be said for New York City;
it is the one densely inhabited locality —
with the possible exception of hell — that
has absolutely not a trace of local pride.
> — *Irvin Cobb*

***
***

Some folks might call me the "night mayor"
of New York.
> — *James J. Walker*

***
***

If there ever was an aviary overstocked
with jays, it is that Yaptown-on-the-Hudson
called New York.
> — *O. Henry*

***
***

Excuse my dust.

— Epitaph, by Dorothy Parker

***
***

I have great faith in fools. Self confidence,
my friends call it.

— Edgar Allan Poe

***
***

The path of civilization is paved with tin cans.

— Elbert Hubbard

***
***

I respect faith, but doubt is what gets you
an education.

— Wilson Mizner

***
***

I say it's spinach, and I say the hell with it.

— E. B. White

***
***

No man can be a patriot on an empty stomach.

— William Cowper Brann

***
***

At twenty a man is full of fight and hope.
He wants to reform the world.
When a man is seventy he still wants to
reform the world, but he knows he can't.

— Clarence Darrow

***
***

The trouble with freedom is that most
people don't know what to do with it.

— Jan Botwinick

***
***

You can always get someone to love you —
even if you have to do it yourself.

— *Tom Masson*

***

I always have trouble remembering three
things; faces, names, and I can't remember
what the third thing is.

— *Fred Allen*

***

If they really want to honor the soldiers,
why don't they let them sit in the stands
and have the people march by?

— *Will Rogers*

A banker is a fellow who lends his
umbrella when the sun is shining,
and wants it back the minute it begins to rain.

— *Mark Twain*

***
***

The first half of our lives is ruined by our
parents and the second half by our children.

— *Clarence Darrow*

***
***

Never get married while you're going
to college; it's hard to get a start
if a prospective employer finds you've
already made one mistake.

— *Kin Hubbard*

***
***

A person who publishes a book willfully
appears in public with his pants down.

— *Edna St. Vincent Millay*

✳✳✳
✳✳✳

"Trees" is one of the most annoying
pieces of verse within my knowledge.
Surely the Kilmer tongue must not have been
very far from the Kilmer cheek when he wrote,
"Poems are made by fools like me."

— *Heywood Broun*

✳✳✳
✳✳✳

Poetry is what Milton saw when he was blind.

— *Don Marquis*

✳✳✳
✳✳✳

I have never been hurt by anything
I didn't say.

— *Calvin Coolidge*

*** ***

It's women's job to keep spiritual entity.
Love can do anything in this world
if they'll just tap it.

— *Adela Rogers St. Johns*

*** ***

Security is an invitation to indolence.

— *Rod McKuen*

*** ***

If you can't stand the heat, get out of
the kitchen.

— *Harry S. Truman*

*** ***

A dog is the only thing on this earth that
loves you more than he loves himself.

— *Josh Billings*

***
***

Manners are the happy way of doing things.

— *Ralph Waldo Emerson*

***
***

I ask not for a larger garden,
but for finer seeds.

— *Russell Conwell*

***
***

There is no more miserable human being than
one in whom nothing is habitual but
indecision.
— *William James*

*** ***

The pursuit of peace is complicated
because it has to do with people,
and nothing in this universe baffles man
as much as man himself.
— *Adlai Stevenson*

*** ***

Genius is one per cent inspiration
and ninety-nine per cent perspiration.
— *Thomas Edison*

I never think of the future.
It comes soon enough.

> — *Albert Einstein*

***
***

It takes your enemy and your friend,
working together, to hurt you:
the one to slander you,
and the other to bring you the news.

> — *Mark Twain*

***
***

I make it a point to seek the company,
intellectually above all, of people who
are superior to me in a number of ways —
and I very often succeed.

> — *Wm. F. Buckley, Jr.*

***
***

To speak ill of others is a dishonest way of
appraising ourselves.

— *Will Durant*

***
***

The world is moving so fast these days
that the man who says it can't be done is
generally interrupted by someone doing it.

— *Elbert Hubbard*

***
***

Among famous traitors of history,
one might mention the weather.

— *Ilka Chase*

***
***

The best service a retired general can perform
is turn in his tongue along with his suit.

— *General Omar Bradley*

***
***

I come from a state that raises corn and cotton and cockleburs and Democrats, and frothy eloquence neither convinces nor satisfies me. I'm from Missouri; you've got to show me.

— *William Duncan Vandiver*

New England has a harsh climate, a barren soil, a rough and stormy coast, and yet we love it, even with a love passing that of dwellers in more favored regions.

— *Henry Cabot Lodge*

I believe that every right implies a
responsibility; every opportunity an
obligation; every possession a duty.

— John D. Rockefeller, Jr.

***
***

We know too much for one man
to know much.

— J. Robert Oppenheimer

***
***

Ours is an age which is proud of machines
that think, and suspicious of any man
who tries to.

— Howard Mumford Jones

***
***

All the ills of democracy can be cured
by more democracy.

— Alfred E. Smith

***
***

Give me your tired, your poor,
Your huddled masses yearning to breathe free,
The wretched refuse of your teaming shore,
Send these, the homeless,
the tempest-tossed to me:
I lift my lamp beside the golden door.

— *Emma Lazarus*

✳✳✳
✳✳✳

I have learned to approach with caution
life's best publicized 'unforgettable moments,'
be they moonshots, love scenes, or funerals.

— *Shana Alexander*

A teacher affects eternity;
he can never tell where his influence stops.

— *Henry Adams*

If you have material things, that's fine.
God has blessed you. But things can be
taken away from you, so you'd best hold on
to the things that mean something,
like nature, or just having each other.

— *June Carter Cash*

It is just as hard to do your duty when
men are sneering at you as when they
are shooting at you.

— *Woodrow Wilson*

An American who speaks French can
only be understood by other Americans
who have also just arrived in Paris.

— *Fred Allen*

A celebrity is one who is known to
many persons he is glad he doesn't know.

— *H. L. Mencken*

✳✳✳
✳✳✳

My mother loved children. She would have given anything if I had been one.

— *Groucho Marx*

***
***

I dislike people who don't believe I am really sick.

— *Oscar Levant*

***
***

No one can make you feel inferior
without your consent.

— *Eleanor Roosevelt*

The hardest thing about prize fighting is
picking up your teeth with a boxing glove.

— *Kin Hubbard*

The difference between a wife and a mistress
is the difference between night and day.

— *Harvey Hershfield*

Beerbohm Tree said what we have all wanted
to say of the extra women in nearly every
throne-room and ballroom and schoolroom
scene since the theatre began. "Ladies,"
said Tree, peering at them plaintively
through his monocle, "just a little more
virginity, if you don't mind."

— *Alexander Woollcott*

✳✳✳
✳✳✳

That's all there is; there isn't any more.

— Ethel Barrymore

***
***